AN ARTIST

AN ARTIST

by M. B. Goffstein

Harper & Row, Publishers

An Artist

Typography by Jane Byers Bierhorst
First Edition

Library of Congress Cataloging in Publication Data
Goffstein, M. B.
An artist.

Summary: Briefly explains how the artist tries
to recreate God's world using his paints.
1. Artists—Psychology—Juvenile literature.
2. Creation (Literary, artistic, etc.)—Juvenile
literature. [1. Artists—Psychology. 2. Creation
(Literary, artistic, etc.)] I. Title.
N71.G58 750'.1'9 79-2663
ISBN 0-06-022012-0
ISBN 0-06-022013-9 lib. bdg.

"Only painting counts."

—PISSARRO

AN ARTIST

An artist is like God,
but small.

He can't see out
of God's creation,

for it includes him.

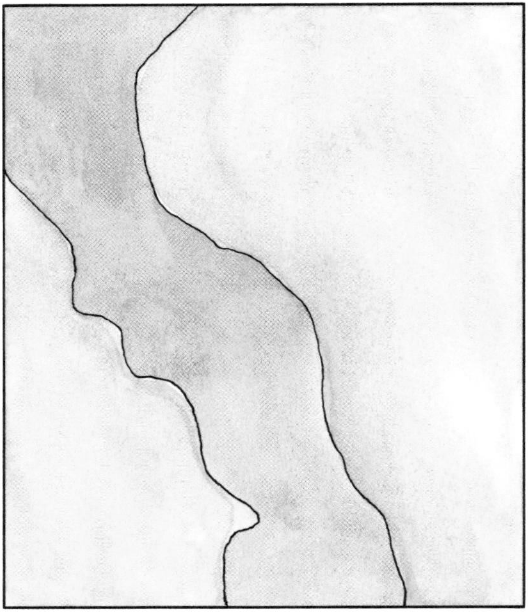

With the seas divided,

all the animals named,

and the sun and moon
and stars

set in their tracks,

an artist spends his life

not only wondering,

but wanting to work
like God

with what he can command:
his paints.

He tries to copy
God's creations.

He tries to shape beauty
with his hand.

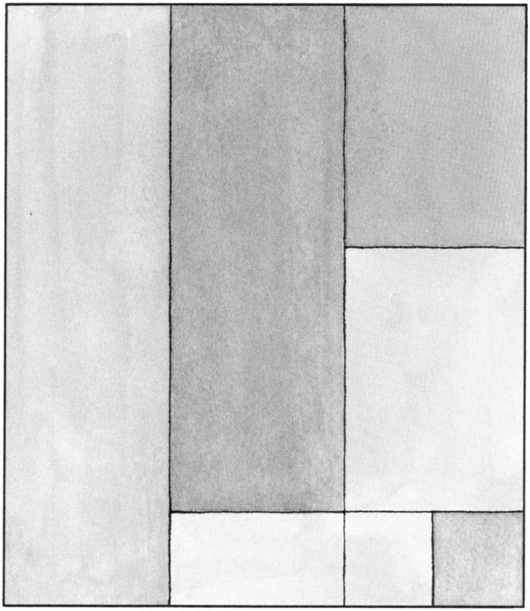

He tries to make order
out of nature.

He tries to paint
the thoughts and feelings
in his mind.

An artist is like God

as God created him.

Small, strong,
and with limited days,

his gift of breath
is spent

over his paintbox.

Choosing and brushing
his colors,

he tries
to make paint sing.